Mystery Beasts

John Townsend

Badger Publishing Limited
Oldmedow Road,
Hardwick Industrial Estate,
King's Lynn PE30 4JJ
Telephone: 01438 791037

www.badgerlearning.co.uk

2 4 6 8 10 9 7 5 3 1

Mystery Beasts ISBN 978-1-78464-008-8

Publisher: Susan Ross
Senior Editor: Danny Pearson
Publishing Assistant: Claire Morgan
Designer: Fiona Grant
Series Consultant: Dee Reid

Photos: Cover Image: © Stocktrek Images, Inc./
Page 7: © Stocktrek Images, Inc./Alamy
Page 10: Sipa Press/REX
Page 11: REX
Page 14: © Dale O'Dell/Alamy
Page 16: © North Wind Picture Archives/Alamy
Page 17: © Amanda Cotton/Alamy
Page 18: © Stocktrek Images, Inc./Alamy
Page 19: Zuma/REX
Page 20: © Stocktrek Images, Inc./Alamy
Page 22: © Stocktrek Images, Inc./Alamy
Page 23: © Felix Choo/Alamy
Page 24: David Beauchamp/REX
Page 25: Times Newspapers/REX
Page 27: © Mark J. Barrett/Alamy
Page 30: © leonello calvetti/Alamy

Attempts to contact all copyright holders have been made.
If any omitted would care to contact Badger Learning, we will be happy to make appropriate arrangements.

Contents

Vocabulary

creature	helicopter
discovering	licence
fake	survive
fuzzy	swerved

Out there and watching us?

There have always been stories of mystery beasts living in wild places.

Every year we find new creatures we didn't know about. Can there still be big mystery beasts out there?

Parts of the world may still hide mystery animals. Get ready to meet a few...

1. Have they all gone?

Dinosaurs died out long ago – or did they? Now and again monsters from the past make the news.

LOCH NESS MONSTER RISES FROM THE DEEP

Man meets dinosaur in swamp

GIANT LIZARD SEEN IN AUSTRALIA

Dinosaur facts:

- Dinosaurs died out about 65 million years ago.
- 'Dinosaur' means 'big lizard'.
- All dinosaurs laid eggs – some of the eggs were 40 centimetres long.

Some people say they have seen a ten metre long lizard (a megalania) in Australia.

Some people think mystery beasts live at the bottom of deep lakes.

For almost 1500 years people have talked about a mystery beast in Scotland.

They say it lives in the deep lake called Loch Ness so it is called the Loch Ness Monster.

The monster is said to be 20 metres long.

This photo of the Loch Ness Monster was taken in 1934. Many years later the photo turned out to be a fake!

This beast is said to live in a huge swamp in Africa.

They call it Mokele Mbembe, which means 'the beast that stops the water'.

2. Wild ape men

Climbers on mountains near Everest say they have seen an ape man in the snow.

People who live there call it the Yeti, which means 'man-beast'.

They say:

- It walks like a human.
- It is two metres tall.
- It has long, dark fur and it smells disgusting.

These footprints are 33 centimetres long.

People say they are the footprints of a Yeti.

Bigfoot

People in wild places in North America say they have seen a mystery beast. They call the mystery beast 'Bigfoot'.

This is a still image from a film a man made in 1967.

He said it shows Bigfoot.

People say this is a Bigfoot footprint.

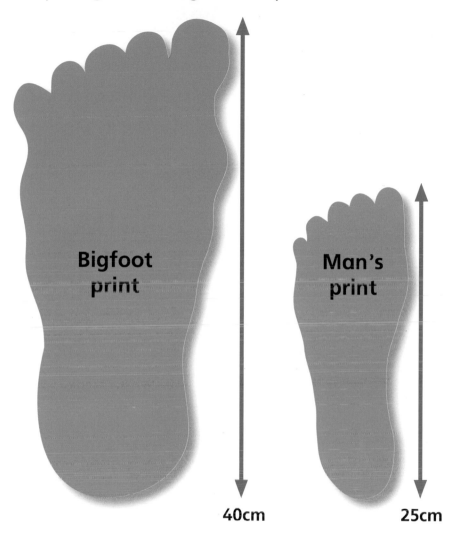

Bigfoot print

Man's print

40cm

25cm

It is much bigger than a human footprint.
Do you think the footprint was made by Bigfoot?
Could it be a fake?

Beware of the Yowie

If you walk in the thick forests of Australia, look out for a Yowie.

Lots of people in Australia say they have seen this mystery 'ape-man'. They say the Yowie is very hairy.

In 2014, a camera in a tree recorded a fuzzy film of a hairy beast. Yowie hunters said it was a Yowie.

In the film you can hear some growling and see some rocks being thrown.

The people said they felt like they were being followed but they were in the middle of nowhere and it was very late at night.

Could it have been a Yowie?

3. Mysteries of the deep

For hundreds of years, sailors have told stories about a huge sea beast called the Kraken.

The sailors said the Kraken had many arms that could reach up from the water and pull ships down to their doom.

Could the Kraken be real?

Maybe the Kraken is really a giant squid.

Giant squid can grow to over 12 metres long.

They sometimes come up from the deep ocean and cling on to ships.

Did those sailors see these huge sea beasts?

Megalodon

Huge dark shadows move under the sea.

Could they be monster sharks?

Some people think a megalodon could still be down there.

Megalodons were the largest hunters in the sea.

They grew to over 20 metres long, which is about four times bigger than a great white shark. Scientists think megalodons died out about two million years ago.

But the oceans are very deep. Maybe giant sharks could still survive. After all, scientists are discovering new fish all the time. So keep looking next time you go swimming!

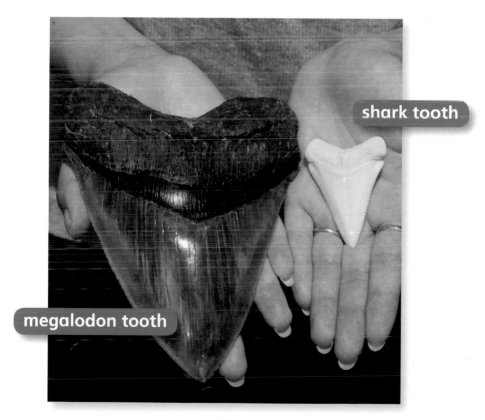

shark tooth

megalodon tooth

4. Flying giants

Millions of years ago, large flying reptiles called pterodactyl flew in the skies. Some people say they still do!

Pterodactyl means 'winged lizard' (a flying reptile).

Some pterodactyl were small, like crows. Some were as big as hang gliders!

In parts of Africa, some people say they have seen a huge flying creature.

They say it looks like a pterodactyl.

The creature attacks people in water so it is called Kongamato, which means 'breaker of boats'.

There are no photos of a Kongamoto.

Do you think it really exists?

Can you believe it?

In 2007, a 29-year-old man crashed his car in the USA.

He told the police he had seen a pterodactyl flying over his car.

When he saw the huge flying creature he swerved off the road and crashed his car.

For hundreds of years, Native Americans have told stories of a giant flying beast.

They called the beast a Thunderbird. They made totem poles showing a Thunderbird.

Could the Thunderbird be a pterodactyl?

5. Alien big cats

The UK has its own mystery beasts. People say there are big cats living in wild parts of the country.

People have reported seeing a big cat in Cornwall.

They call it the Beast of Bodmin Moor and they say that it kills farm animals.

Is there really a Beast of Bodmin Moor?

In 1995, a large skull with fangs was found on Bodmin Moor. It was the skull of a leopard.

Guess what!
Experts worked out the skull had come from a leopard-skin rug.

The animal hadn't died in Britain, after all!

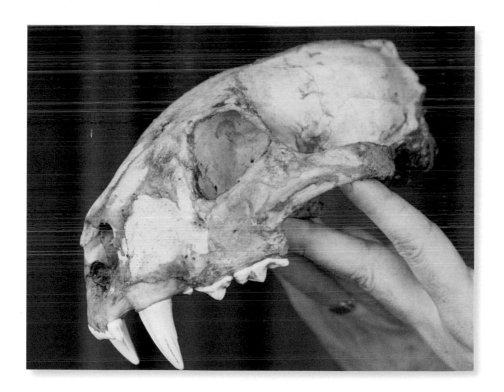

UK big cats

If big cats live wild in Britain, how did they get there?

Maybe they were once pets. If they escaped, they could survive by hunting in the wild.

WOW! facts

Years ago, some people kept big cats as pets. They even walked them in the street.

But in 1974, a leopard killed a child so the law was changed. People with big cats had to buy a licence.

Some people couldn't pay for the licence – so maybe they let their big cats go... into the woods.

In Wales, when sheep are attacked, some people say they have been killed by a big cat.

Of course, the sheep could have been killed by dogs or foxes but a big cat makes a much better story!

Guess what!
Some big cat sightings have turned out to be pet cats or even stuffed toys.

In Southampton, an army helicopter search found a mystery beast was really a life-size toy tiger!

NEARLY ONE BIG CAT SIGHTING A WEEK REPORTED TO POLICE LAST YEAR

(The Sun Newspaper in 2014)

- **Across the UK, people report seeing leopards, panthers and pumas in the wild.**

- **A jogger claimed he saw two big cats at least a metre tall chasing three deer near Grimsby.**

Leopards have been reported in the UK. You could say they've been 'spotted'!

6. Real or fake?

Some strange animals were once thought to be fake.

The duck-billed platypus of Australia was a puzzle to scientists. This mammal is like a beaver but it lays eggs and has a beak.

People thought some other animals had been sewn together for a joke! We now know they are very real.

Questions

What does the word 'dinosaur' mean? *(page 7)*

How tall is the Yeti reported to be? *(page 10)*

When do scientists think megalodons died out? *(page 19)*

Are there any real photos of the Kongamoto? *(page 21)*

What year was a large skull with fangs found on Bodmin Moor? *(page 25)*

How often is there a big cat sighting in the UK? *(page 29)*

Index